THE SILENT SELKIE

The Silent Selkie describes a character who is unable to communicate in words and whose only way of communicating is through the weather, which leads to disastrous consequences not only for the Selkie, but also for everyone around her.

But behind her golden scales, the Selkie hides a secret wound that even she is unaware of, and it is only when the Selkie's skin becomes uncovered by the force of the sea that she remembers the terrible story of what caused her hurt, long ago. Only then can the Selkie come to terms with her wound and begin a journey of healing that will bring her face-to-face with what she has needed all along.

Beautifully illustrated and sensitively written, *The Silent Selkie* deals with the effects of trauma on a young person – including hypersensitivity and emotional reactivity. The story uses the metaphor of trauma as a 'hidden wound', which in reality is an emotional or psychological pain that needs both acknowledgement and expression, within the context of a safe, supportive environment, in which to begin to heal.

This colourful storybook:

- Helps adults provide a safe environment for children to use non-verbal expression to communicate experiences that may be difficult to talk about.

- Uses creative metaphors and symbols to offer children a supportive way to communicate, whilst maintaining a safe distance from the source of their emotional pain.

- Inspires and empowers children to begin their journey of healing.

The Silent Selkie encourages young people who may have adverse childhood experiences or trauma to develop greater understanding of how this can affect them and is ideal reading for those working with vulnerable children and young people seeking to use the expressive arts to develop greater emotional literacy in children with a background of trauma.

Juliette Ttofa is a specialist educational psychologist and child therapist with a long-standing interest in the complex issues surrounding trauma, attachment needs and emotional resilience.

'An excellent contribution and resource for those working with the troubled child. This hauntingly beautiful story will appeal to many children who have suffered from a variety of traumatic experiences. It will help them to make sense of their situation and reassure them that they are not alone in their inner pain. The accompanying guidebook will provide understanding of adverse childhood experiences and offer valuable skills and ideas for the adult who wishes to work alongside such children in a creative way.'

Eunice Stagg, *President – Association for Sandplay Therapy. BACP Snr Accredited Counsellor, Essex, UK*

The Silent Selkie

Written by

Juliette Ttofa

Illustrated by

Paul Greenhouse

Routledge
Taylor & Francis Group

LONDON AND NEW YORK

Cover image @ Paul Greenhouse

First published 2022
by Routledge
4 Park Square, Milton Park, Abingdon, Oxon OX14 4RN

and by Routledge
605 Third Avenue, New York, NY 10158

Routledge is an imprint of the Taylor & Francis Group, an informa business

British Library Cataloguing-in-Publication Data
A catalogue record for this book is available from the British Library

Library of Congress Cataloging-in-Publication Data
A catalog record for this book has been requested

ISBN: 978-0-367-63949-5 (pbk)
ISBN: 978-1-003-12145-9 (ebk)

DOI: 10.4324/9781003121459

Typeset in Calibri
by Apex CoVantage, LLC

For Anna

Somewhere in the vastness of space, below a midnight sky of infinite stars, deep under a dark green sea,

there lived a silent Selkie with seal-like skin and scales of gold …

… and the heart of weather.

When the Selkie was sad, the dark clouds would gather.

When the Selkie was upset, the clouds would burst with rain.

And when the Selkie was cross, the winds would howl around and around like a band of wolves.

Then, there were times when the Selkie was enraged beyond all containment and the night would explode in a terrible storm.

So, one day, the seal-folk surrounded the silent Selkie and asked: "Why do you act in such ways?"

But the Selkie could not say.

She turned away, flicking her tail like a scorpion's sting, and sent a blast of sand into their eyes.

"Enough is enough!" the seal-folk decided.

They banished the Selkie to a faraway cave and told her to stay there for her own safety.

There the Selkie remained day after day, for week upon week …

A fog descended over the cave and the Selkie's hair grew longer and longer, until she became a wild thing.

One night as the Selkie slept, her dreams made her restless.

She tossed and turned so much that her wild hair floated to the surface of the ocean and was tugged by the tide above.

But the Selkie's rebellious hair was so unruly that it became snagged in a fishing net.

And, suddenly she was pulled out from the cave.

The other seal-folk saw what had happened and tried to call out, "Selkie, wake up!"

But the Selkie did not wake.

The fishing trawler dragged the Selkie for miles and miles across the sea to a land unknown.

When the Selkie awoke, she had been washed up on the sandy shoreline of a strange island.

Several of Selkie's golden scales had been dislodged revealing patches of skin.

Still ensnared in fish-net, a full sun blazed down upon the Selkie and her golden scales began to burn like fire.

The Selkie struggled to free herself from the net, but it was no good.

She checked her image in a slice of polished stone.

The Selkie sighed. Her face was drawn and her large tail-fin was limp.

Then small chinks in her golden scales became visible.

She gasped out loud. But there was something else...

As she smoothed her hand over her newly uncovered skin, she felt a needle bristle against her fingertips.

Then the Selkie saw it:
a tiny splinter.

"How long have I had this spine in my side?" the Selkie silently wondered.

Just as soon as the Selkie had noticed the thorn, she began to feel it. The barbed point had punctured and pierced her flesh making it throb.

The Selkie screamed out in pain.

"What is it?" squawked a passing Razorbill.

The Selkie pointed to her side and offered the Razorbill one of her golden scales to remove the splinter.

The Razorbill understood. And, after taking the gold from the Selkie, the Razorbill pecked at the spike with its huge beak.

The Selkie's skin became bruised and raw, and she cried out.

"Well, it is going to hurt," the Razorbill said unkindly. "It has been stuck in your body for a long time."

But the Selkie turned her body away from the Razorbill and would not let it peck at her skin anymore.

"Suit yourself," the Razorbill replied indignantly, and flew off with its treasure, leaving the Selkie in more pain than before.

The Selkie began to screech and the sea creatures around her slunk away. All except one.

"There now, I can help you," the creature hissed. It was a Knifefish.

"I can remove the pain in your voice," the Knifefish said.

The Selkie offered the Knifefish two of her golden scales.

So, the Knifefish took them and slid its body
towards the Selkie.

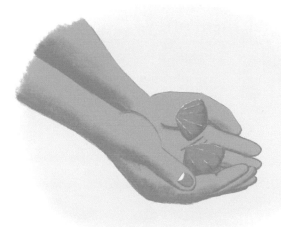

"Close your eyes," the Knifefish urged. "Hold still now…"

The Selkie shut her eyes tightly and braced herself.

Then she felt a stinging jolt.

The Knifefish had stunned the Selkie's throat with its
electric charge.

The Selkie tried to cry out but her voice was stifled and only a
thin sound issued from her mouth.

Meanwhile, the eel had slithered away with its treasure of gold.
The Selkie sobbed silently.
Under the fiery sun's ferocious glare, her golden scales had
become scorching hot.
So the Selkie began to pick them off.

She cast the scales into the sea one by one
and they scattered on the surface of the
water, leaving a winding trail of gold…

The Selkie grabbed a nearby shell and used it as a mouthpiece for her tiny voice.

She called through the horn with all her might. But the sky was dark and empty, and the sea was hushed still. And no one came to her rescue.

Looking almost human, the Selkie curled up into a ball and fell asleep.

Then the night became long and dark and cold for the Selkie.

For that night, as the Selkie slept, her body remembered…all that she had forgotten.

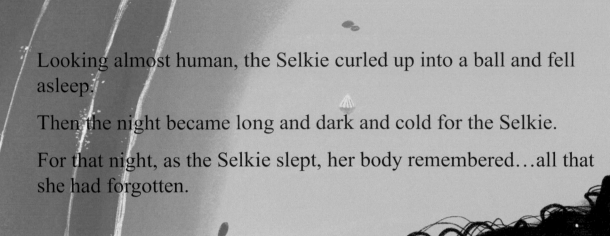

The terrible story of how the thorn had become implanted in her skin long ago, when she was just a seal-pup and her skin was soft and supple.

And in her half-dreams, the Selkie began to moan strange sounds.

Sounds, like a song that made no sense to anyone.

Her song echoed deep under a dark green sea,
below the midnight sky of infinite stars
and into the vastness of space…

Above the Selkie, the sky began to billow in the breeze like a curtain
of stardust and the clouds glistened like drifts of night-time snow.

As she awoke the next morning, even the new day brought no hope and she fell weakly towards the shoreline.

But as she dropped to the sand,
suddenly the Selkie felt it…

A burst of cooling sea spray.

The Selkie shook her head and opened her eyes brightly towards the sunlit sea.

Emerging from the deep was a beautiful humpback whale.

Each day after that, the same whale visited the Selkie,
gradually coming closer and closer to the shore.

It sang with the Selkie and delivered up a spray of salty
sea water to soothe her splintered skin.

Then one day, there was not just one whale, but a whole school of mighty whales – all singing a whale-song that matched the Selkie's own strange tune.

The creatures thumped the ocean with their formidable fins, until the Selkie was released from her fish-net and at last could swim back into the sea.

Her body softened. She felt safe. She felt free.

And she spoke.

"Why have I never felt this way before?" the Selkie asked.

"Young Selkie," the wise whale said kindly. "You have
had a hidden wound hurting you for so long that you have not dared
to feel."

"Encased in your golden plated armour, you have locked away all
that you felt until it escaped like a dangerous convict from behind
the bars of a prison cell".

"But your golden shell also concealed all that is good and strong and
powerful in you."

"Your story is not over Selkie," the whale smiled, giving the Selkie a golden crown. "It is time for you to be who you really are."

The Selkie nodded.

"It will not be easy," said the whale.
"But you are not alone."

The Selkie looked cautiously towards the splinter in her side, ready to remove it.

But it was no longer there.

All that remained was a faint scar.
in a shimmering new skin…

… and a heart that dared to feel.